DREAM JOBS IN ENGINEERING

COLIN HYNSON

NASA 1 X-43A

Crabtree Publishing Company
www.crabtreebooks.com

Crabtree Publishing Company

www.crabtreebooks.com

1-800-387-7650

Published in Canada
616 Welland Ave.
St. Catharines, ON
L2M 5V6

Published in the United States
PMB 59051
350 Fifth Ave. 59th Floor
New York, NY

Published in 2017 by CRABTREE PUBLISHING COMPANY

First published in 2016 by Wayland
(A division of Hachette Children's Books)
Copyright © Wayland 2016

Author:
Colin Hynson

Editors:
Victoria Brooker
Jon Richards
Petrice Custance

Designer:
Darren Jordan

Proofreader:
Wendy Scavuzzo

Print and production coordinator:
Katherine Berti

Photo credits

1, 26bl courtesy of NASA, 2, 12–13 Dreamstime.com/Mikhail Druzhinin, 3, 23b Dreamstime.com/Piccaya, 4–5 Dreamstime.com/Gleres, 5tr Dreamstime.com/Lunamarina, 5cr Dreamstime.com/Alexander Sandvoss, 6–7 Dreamstime.com/Freestyleimages, 7tl Dreamstime.com/Viachelav Iacobchuk, 8cl Dreamstime.com/Cylonphoto, 8–9 Dreamstime.com/Stockr, 10cl Dreamstime.com/Delfinista, 10–11 Dreamstime.com/Alexander Sandvoss, 11tr Dreamstime.com/Ivan23g, 12cl Dreamstime.com/Belahoche, 14cl Citypeek Creative Commons Sharealike, 14–15 Dreamstime.com/Pichit Boonhuad, 16bl Dreamstime.com/Jasminko Ibrakovic, 16–17 Dreamstime.com/James Frecker, 18bl, 31br Dreamstime.com/Bai Xuejia, 18–19 Dreamstime.com/ Péter Gudella, 19cl Dreamstime.com/Piero Crucciati, 20–21 Dreamstime.com/Maren Winter, 22cl Dreamstime.com/ProductionPerig, 24bl FlickrLickr Creative Commons Sharealike, 24–25 Dreamstime.com/Grigor Atanasov, 26–27 Dreamstime.com/Boarding1now, 27tl courtesy of NASA, 28–29 Dreamstime.com/Martine De Graaf

Library and Archives Canada Cataloguing in Publication

Hynson, Colin, author
Dream jobs in engineering / Colin Hynson.

(Cutting-edge careers in STEM)
Issued in print and electronic formats.
ISBN 978-0-7787-2945-7 (hardback).--ISBN 978-0-7787-2969-3 (paperback).--
ISBN 978-1-4271-1860-8 (html)

1. Engineering--Vocational guidance--Juvenile literature.
I. Title.

TA157.H96 2016   j620.0023   C2016-906636-3
                                           C2016-906637-1

Library of Congress Cataloging-in-Publication Data

CIP available at the Library of Congress.

Printed in Hong Kong/012017/BK20161024

CONTENTS

ENGINEERING

JOBS IN ENGINEERING

QUALIFICATIONS IN ENGINEERING CAN TAKE YOU FROM THE DEPTHS OF EARTH TO TOWERS THAT SOAR HIGH INTO THE SKY.

Welcome to the world of working in engineering. Studying engineering can open doors to a whole range of interesting, exciting, unusual, and amazing jobs in engineering. A career in engineering doesn't mean you'll be stuck on a construction site. You could have a job in robotics, motor sports, or 3-D printing, just to name a few. This book will help you find out what kinds of engineering jobs are out there, as well as the rewards of doing the job.

▼ Creating a terrifying **amusement park** ride requires a detailed understanding of forces and the strength of materials.

SUBJECTS AND QUALIFICATIONS

For each job, you'll find out what subjects you may need to study as you move through school, and what further training you will need. These are quite general because what you study for a particular job will change depending on which country you are in.

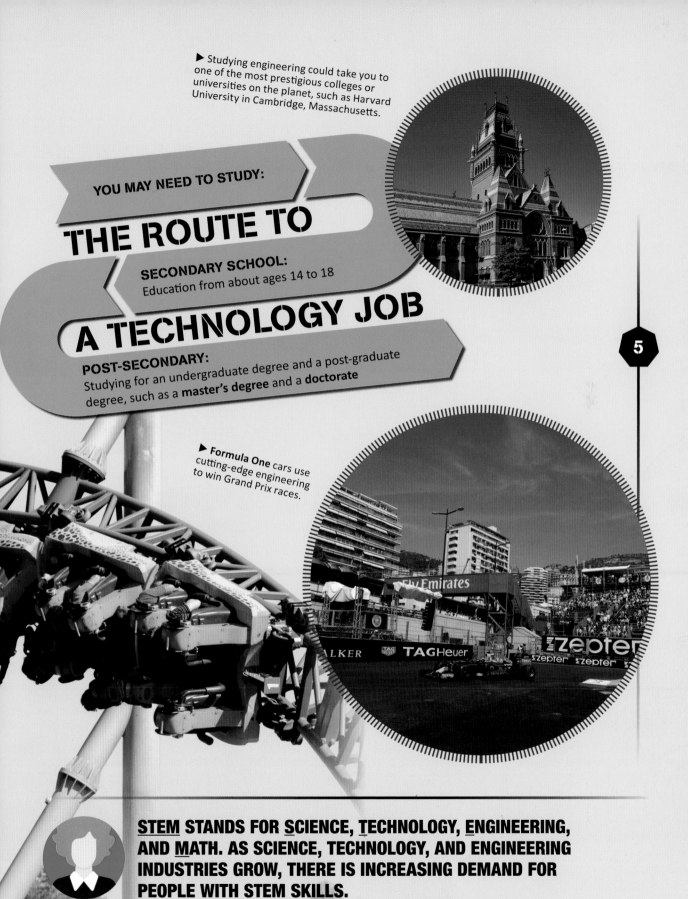

▶ Studying engineering could take you to one of the most prestigious colleges or universities on the planet, such as Harvard University in Cambridge, Massachusetts.

YOU MAY NEED TO STUDY:

THE ROUTE TO

SECONDARY SCHOOL:
Education from about ages 14 to 18

A TECHNOLOGY JOB

POST-SECONDARY:
Studying for an undergraduate degree and a post-graduate degree, such as a **master's degree** and a **doctorate**

▶ **Formula One** cars use cutting-edge engineering to win Grand Prix races.

<u>S</u>TEM STANDS FOR <u>S</u>CIENCE, <u>T</u>ECHNOLOGY, <u>E</u>NGINEERING, AND <u>M</u>ATH. AS SCIENCE, TECHNOLOGY, AND ENGINEERING INDUSTRIES GROW, THERE IS INCREASING DEMAND FOR PEOPLE WITH STEM SKILLS.

PRINTING IN 3-D

THIS TECHNOLOGY ALLOWS YOU TO MAKE WHAT YOU WANT, WHEN YOU WANT IT.

3-D PRINTING USES A WIDE RANGE OF MATERIALS INCLUDING PLASTIC, CLAY, METAL, RUBBER, AND EVEN FOOD.

Also known as "**additive manufacturing**," 3-D printing allows businesses to create new products easily, without having to build expensive prototypes. The method can also be used to make a small number of the product to see if people are interested in buying it. Even though it is still quite a new industry, 3-D printing is being used in a wide range of industries, including car and aircraft building, and even creating new body parts.

◀ A digital model of the item is created on a computer before the 3-D printers get to work.

WHAT YOU DO

Working as a 3-D printing engineer, you will be involved in the process of creating a new product from start to finish. You'll spend much of your day making sure that the 3-D printer is ready to start working and that the materials being used are also available. You'll be working as part of a team including designers and computer coders who use Computer–Aided Design (CAD) software.

At the moment, most people in 3-D printing work with engineering companies or in aerospace and healthcare. However, the range of businesses that are looking to use 3-D printing is expanding fast. One growth area is in electrical engineering, where 3-D printing can be used to create electrical circuits.

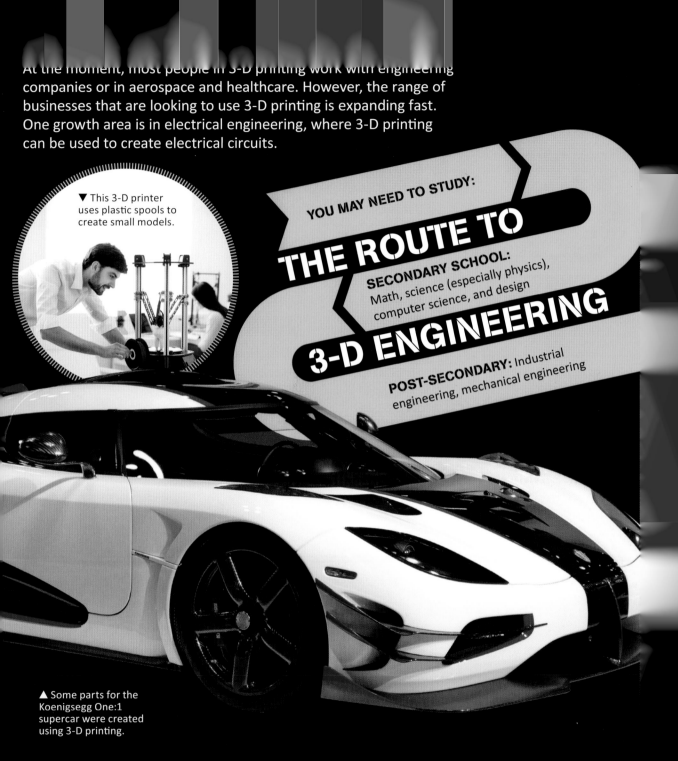

▼ This 3-D printer uses plastic spools to create small models.

YOU MAY NEED TO STUDY:

THE ROUTE TO
3-D ENGINEERING

SECONDARY SCHOOL: Math, science (especially physics), computer science, and design

POST-SECONDARY: Industrial engineering, mechanical engineering

▲ Some parts for the Koenigsegg One:1 supercar were created using 3-D printing.

NASA IS SEEING IF 3-D PRINTING CAN CREATE ENTIRE MEALS FOR ASTRONAUTS. THAT WAY THEY CAN MAKE SURE THAT ASTRONAUTS ARE GETTING TASTY AND NUTRITIOUS FOOD.

GREEN ENGINEERING

PLAY YOUR PART IN SAVING THE PLANET BY USING YOUR ENGINEERING QUALIFICATIONS TO KEEP THINGS GREEN.

One of the greatest challenges facing people today is the issue of **climate change**. We are producing millions of tons of **greenhouse gases** every year and many people believe that it's changing our climate and making our planet warmer. To try to reduce the impact, many countries are developing renewable sources of energy. This includes producing electricity from wind, sunlight, and water.

◄ Engineers inspect the huge **turbines** in a **hydroelectric power** plant.

WHAT YOU DO

As a **renewable energy** engineer, you will spend some of your time working in a laboratory designing and researching renewable energy projects. This will mean creating computer models and carrying out experiments. You will also spend time working outside choosing places to build a **wind turbine** or a **solar farm** and returning to the area when building starts. If you're designing an off–shore wind turbine, then you will be going out to sea.

AN AREA OF RENEWABLE ENERGY ENGINEERING THAT NEEDS MORE RESEARCH IS IN THE STORAGE OF ENERGY. AT THIS TIME, STORING POWER IS NOT EASY, AND COMPANIES ARE TRYING TO DEVELOP BETTER WAYS OF DOING THIS.

THE IVANPAH SOLAR ELECTRIC GENERATING SYSTEM IN CALIFORNIA COVERS 3,707 ACRES (1,500 HECTARES) AND CAN GENERATE ENOUGH POWER FOR NEARLY 140,000 HOMES.

◀ Gigantic turbines stand high above the ground to make the most of the wind.

WHERE YOU WORK
Engineers working in renewable energy will work for businesses that design, build, and install the machinery needed to capture energy. Many businesses usually concentrate on just one kind of renewable energy, so you can choose whether you want to work in wind, solar, or hydropower.

YOU MAY NEED TO STUDY:

THE ROUTE TO

SECONDARY SCHOOL:
Math, science (especially physics), computer science, and engineering

RENEWABLE

POST-SECONDARY: Mechanical engineering or electrical engineering. Some colleges and universities offer courses in environmental engineering.

ENERGY ENGINEERING

RACE ENGINEER

ENGINEERING QUALIFICATIONS CAN TAKE YOU INTO THE SUPER-FAST WORLD OF MOTORSPORTS.

For fans of car racing, there is nothing as exciting as a Formula One race. The drivers competing against each other in **Grand Prix** races are in cars that often reach speeds of more than 220 mph (350 kph). One of the most important members of every race team is the race engineer. As a race engineer, your main job will be to make sure that the car is set up to suit conditions and tactics, and that it performs at its best during the race.

▲ The data you collect and study from the onboard computers will tell the team of mechanics how to set up different parts of the car, including the **aerodynamic** wings.

WHAT YOU DO

Outside of the race season, you will be involved in developing and testing the car for the next season. When the races begin, your job will involve setting the car up for practice and qualification, checking data from onboard computers to see how it performs, and deciding with the team how to get the most out of the car.

▶ Throughout the race, race engineers listen to the driver to find out how the car is handling.

ALL KINDS OF MOTORSPORTS USE RACE ENGINEERS. YOU COULD WORK AT RACING EVENTS SUCH AS THE MOTOGP, KART RACING, OR LONG-DISTANCE RALLIES.

WHERE YOU WORK

The companies that build Formula One cars are called "constructors" and many of the best race engineers work for one of them. However, you could choose to work for a company that provides engines or other parts for the constructors.

▲ Talking to the driver before and after the race and between practice sessions could help you extract more performance from the car.

YOU MAY NEED TO STUDY:

THE ROUTE TO

SECONDARY SCHOOL: Math, science (especially physics), computer science, and engineering

RACE ENGINEERING

POST-SECONDARY: Mechanical engineering, automotive engineering, or electrical engineering

MAKING BODY PARTS

BUILDING AND ENGINEERING NEW AND REPLACEMENT BODY PARTS CAN HELP PEOPLE REBUILD THEIR LIVES.

Bioengineers help to design and build artificial replacements for body parts that are either missing or not functioning properly. One of the main areas that bioengineers work in is the development of artificial limbs. These are called **prosthetics**. Some prosthetics even have electronics in them that can react to instructions given to them by the wearer. Engineers are also trying to develop artificial limbs that can respond to the wearer's thoughts.

◀ An engineer adjusts the settings on a prosthetic leg in the laboratory before it is sent to the person who will wear it.

SOME PEOPLE WITH DISABILITIES STILL TAKE PART IN SPORTS. IF YOU WANT TO WORK IN SPORTS AND BIOENGINEERING, YOU CAN BE INVOLVED IN THE DEVELOPMENT OF SPECIALIZED ARTIFICIAL LIMBS USED BY ATHLETES.

IT IS NOW POSSIBLE TO REPLACE OTHER PARTS OF THE BODY, INCLUDING INTERNAL ORGANS SUCH AS THE HEART, LIVER, AND KIDNEYS. BIOENGINEERS ARE ALSO WORKING ON REPLACEMENTS FOR SKIN, INTESTINES, AND BONES.

WHAT YOU DO

Most of your working day will be spent in the laboratory working as part of a team researching and developing artificial body parts. Some of your day, however, may be spent away from the laboratory, meeting with the patients and the medical team who are working with the body parts.

WHERE YOU WORK

It is likely you will be working for a healthcare company that creates artificial body parts. You could also be working for hospitals or for medical schools that specialize in bioengineering.

◀ A sprinter with a specially designed prosthetic running leg takes off at the start of a race.

THE ROUTE

YOU MAY NEED TO STUDY:

SECONDARY SCHOOL: Math, science (especially biology), computer science, and engineering

TO BIOENGINEERING

POST-SECONDARY: Biomedical engineering or mechanical engineering

DRILLING ENGINEER

FIND OUT WHAT IT TAKES TO DRILL DEEP INTO EARTH'S INTERIOR.

THE DEEPEST FLOATING OIL PLATFORM IS THE *PERDIDO* WHICH SITS IN 8,038 FEET (2,450 METERS) OF WATER IN THE GULF OF MEXICO.

The world needs energy and, at the moment, more thab half of all our energy comes from oil and gas. Both are buried in large underground fields and have to be extracted by drilling. As a drilling engineer, you will help to discover these new fields around the world. This means that you will have to have some knowledge of **geology**. You will then need to organize test drillings and, if these are successful, you will be involved in building the wells needed to bring the oil and gas to the surface.

▲ A drilling engineer analyzes the earth and rock brought up by drilling and keeps a record in a "**mud log**."

WHAT YOU DO

The working day of a drilling engineer may take you to many different parts of the world since you will be responsible for building wells. Oil and gas fields are being found in some of the most challenging environments in the world. Many of the new fields have been found out at sea, so you will probably spend some of your time on an oil or gas platform far from land.

DRILLING ENGINEERS ARE ALSO INVOLVED IN TRYING TO MEET THE WORLD'S INCREASING DEMAND FOR WATER. THIS WATER IS OFTEN FOUND BY DRILLING INTO UNDERGROUND SOURCES OF WATER CALLED AQUIFERS.

▼ Drilling platforms can be found far out at sea, boring through the ocean floor to reach the oil and gas.

WHERE YOU WORK
The exploration of new oil and gas fields is mostly in the hands of big energy companies. They are continually searching for new fields around the world, and most drilling engineers work for one of these big companies. There are also some smaller companies who specialize in the design and building of oil and gas wells.

15

THE ROUTE
YOU MAY NEED TO STUDY:

SECONDARY SCHOOL: Math, science (especially biology), geography, and engineering

TO DRILLING ENGINEER

POST-SECONDARY: Petroleum engineering, mechanical engineering, or civil engineering

RUNNING SHOE ENGINEER

CAN YOU ENGINEER THE NEXT BIG THING IN SPORTS EQUIPMENT?

If you want to be a top athlete, you'll need to be fit and healthy and ready to put in the practice. However, a lot of athletes are also turning to technology to help improve their performance and engineers can help, especially when it comes to what athletes wear on their feet. As a running shoe engineer, you'll be involved in creating general purpose shoes for the everyday runner, as well as specialized footwear for elite athletes in different sports.

▲ A good general running shoe should support the athlete's foot and provide cushioning to absorb impact.

◄ Studying how a person runs is called **gait analysis** and it will help you to create shoes that could improve their performance.

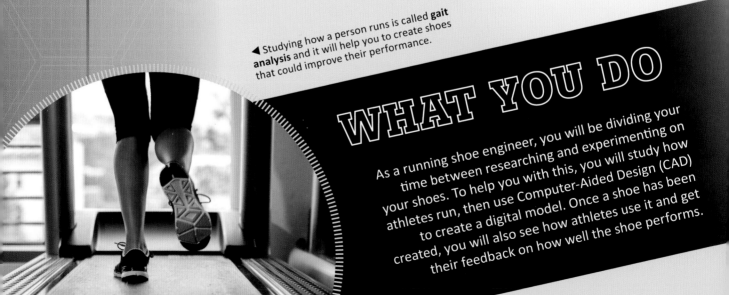

WHAT YOU DO

As a running shoe engineer, you will be dividing your time between researching and experimenting on your shoes. To help you with this, you will study how athletes run, then use Computer-Aided Design (CAD) to create a digital model. Once a shoe has been created, you will also see how athletes use it and get their feedback on how well the shoe performs.

BY 2018, THE GLOBAL ATHLETICS SHOE MARKET MAY BE WORTH NEARLY $84 BILLION.

WHERE YOU WORK

Most running shoe engineers work for one of the large companies that design and manufacture all sorts of sports clothes and equipment. Many of these companies have offices across the globe, so you may find yourself working in different countries.

THE ROUTE TO

YOU MAY NEED TO STUDY:

SECONDARY SCHOOL: Math, science (especially biology and physics), engineering, and design

RUNNING SHOE ENGINEERING

POST-SECONDARY: Sports engineering or mechanical engineering

A CAREER IN SPORTS ENGINEERING COULD LEAD TO A JOB WORKING WITH ALL SORTS OF SPORTS EQUIPMENT, INCLUDING IMPROVING TENNIS RACKETS OR MAKING SWIMSUITS THAT REDUCE FRICTION.

MAKING TOYS

IF YOU BELIEVED PLAYTIME STOPPED WHEN YOU GREW UP, THIS JOB WILL MAKE YOU THINK AGAIN!

18

When a toy is designed and built, someone with engineering skills will be part of the team. As a toy engineer, you will be involved in making sure that all parts of the toy work efficiently and that the toy itself is fun to use. One of your most important jobs will be to use your engineering skills to make sure that any new toys are safe. It will be up to you to make sure no small parts can be taken off the toy and swallowed.

◀ Many modern toys use computer chips that allow them to interact with their owners.

◀ The Rubik's Cube was created by architecture professor Ernõ Rubik to help his students understand 3-D objects.

AS A TOY ENGINEER, YOU MAY BE ABLE TO SPECIALIZE IN THE KIND OF TOYS BEING CREATED. YOU MIGHT WANT TO JUST CONCENTRATE ON ACTION TOYS OR TOYS FOR BABIES.

THE ROUTE TO

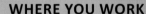

YOU MAY NEED TO STUDY:

SECONDARY SCHOOL: Math, science (especially physics), engineering, and design

TOY ENGINEERING

POST-SECONDARY: Electrical engineering or mechanical engineering

WHERE YOU WORK

If you want to work in toy engineering, you will probably work for a toy manufacturer. Many of these businesses are creating toys that can be sold all over the world, so you will have the chance to work in several different countries. There are also some companies that design toys, but do not make them. If you work for one of these companies, you will be part of a team that will try to sell the designs to a toy manufacturer.

▼ A toy fair is a good place to see the other toys appearing on the market.

WHAT YOU DO

If you are developing a new toy, you will be part of a team that works closely together through every stage in the creation of the toy. When you are working on the design of the toy, you will be using a computer to help you with your work. Once you are testing the toy, you'll spend much more time in a laboratory or in toy stores watching how children use your creations.

BUILDING SHIPS

POWERING THE SHIPS THAT SAIL AROUND THE GLOBE TAKES SOME SUPER-ADVANCED ENGINEERING.

There are a lot of types of ships out at sea right now. These include bulk carriers, cargo and container ships, tankers carrying oil and gas, and enormous cruise ships. All of these ships need the skills of an engineer to keep them running efficiently and safely. As a ship engineer, you will be involved in designing and building new ships, ensuring that they can perform safely and efficiently.

▼ As well as building new ships, your role may involve repairing or refitting existing ships to bring them up to date.

◄ Many ships are built in sections that are then joined together at a **shipyard**.

WHAT YOU DO

When you are at the initial design stage of engineering a ship, you will be based in an office using CAD software. However, you will also have to spend a lot of time away from your desk supervising the building, maintenance, or repair of ships at the shipyard.

IF YOU WANT TO BE RESPONSIBLE FOR THE DESIGN OF THE WHOLE SHIP, YOU WILL HAVE TO RETURN TO UNIVERSITY TO STUDY MARINE ENGINEERING AT A HIGHER LEVEL.

WHERE YOU WORK

Most ship engineers work for ship building companies that are based at shipyards. You could also work for companies that specialize in the repair and maintenance of ships. Countries with large navies, such as the United States Navy or the Royal Navy in the UK, employ engineers to work on their ships.

YOU MAY NEED TO STUDY:

THE ROUTE TO

SECONDARY SCHOOL: Math, science (especially physics), engineering, and design

BUILDING SHIPS

POST-SECONDARY: Marine engineering, electrical engineering, or mechanical engineering

SKYSCRAPER ENGINEERING

THIS JOB WILL LET YOU REACH FOR THE SKY AS YOU CREATE SOME OF THE WORLD'S TALLEST BUILDINGS.

Major cities around the world build towering skyscrapers to create more living and working space. These huge buildings provide massive engineering challenges. As a skyscraper engineer, your most important task is to make sure that the skyscraper stays standing after it's built. You will have to understand how the building's materials will stand up to the natural conditions high above the city streets.

THE HEIGHT OF ONE WORLD TRADE CENTER IN NEW YORK CITY IS 1,776 FEET (541 METERS). IT IS THE TALLEST BUILDING IN NORTH AMERICA.

▲ You will work closely with the **architect** to make sure the building fulfills their vision and is safe to use.

WHAT YOU DO

At the start of a project, you will be spending your time in your office using a computer to work on the design of every part of the skyscraper. You will also set up computer models to test the parts of the skyscraper you are responsible for. Some testing will also have to be done in a laboratory. When the skyscraper is being built, you will have to be on site to help supervise the engineering work needed.

THERE ARE MANY SPECIALIST ROLES INVOLVED IN BUILDING A SKYSCRAPER. THESE INCLUDE DESIGNING THE ELEVATORS, AIR CONDITIONING, LIGHTING, AND THE SUPPLY OF WATER TO ALL FLOORS.

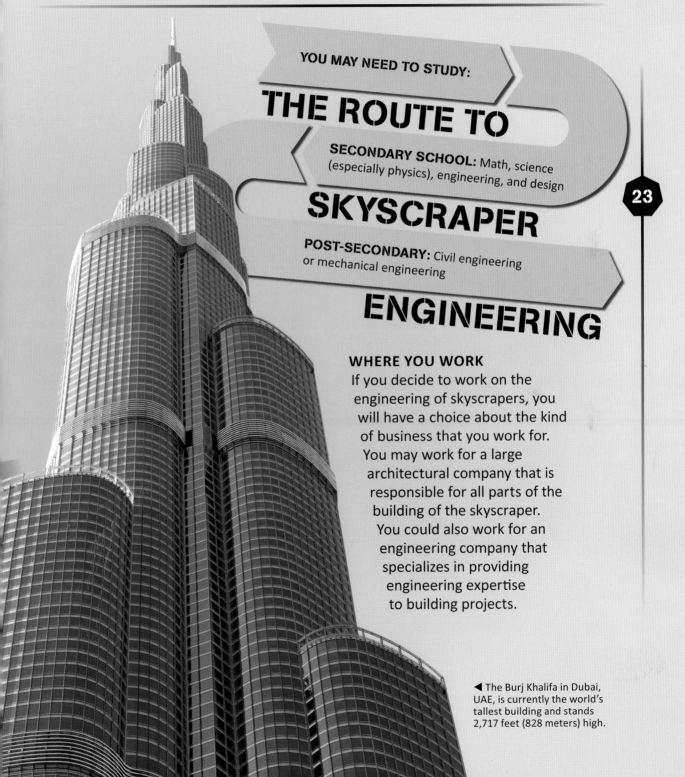

YOU MAY NEED TO STUDY:

THE ROUTE TO

SECONDARY SCHOOL: Math, science (especially physics), engineering, and design

SKYSCRAPER

POST-SECONDARY: Civil engineering or mechanical engineering

ENGINEERING

WHERE YOU WORK

If you decide to work on the engineering of skyscrapers, you will have a choice about the kind of business that you work for. You may work for a large architectural company that is responsible for all parts of the building of the skyscraper. You could also work for an engineering company that specializes in providing engineering expertise to building projects.

◀ The Burj Khalifa in Dubai, UAE, is currently the world's tallest building and stands 2,717 feet (828 meters) high.

ROLLER COASTERS

IF ROLLER COASTER THRILLS ARE YOUR THING, THIS IS THE JOB FOR YOU!

As a roller coaster engineer, you will have to decide what the roller coaster will look like. That means making decisions about the height of any drops, whether there will be any water or tunnels, and if there are going to be any vertical loops. You will have to use your engineering skills to decide on the speed limit of the cars on the roller coaster. You'll need an understanding of how the materials used on the roller coaster work. You will also need a good knowledge of physics, and even know something about the human body.

◀ Some modern roller coasters are built using traditional materials, such as wood.

WHAT YOU DO

Although you will spend some time in the office working on the design of the roller coaster, you will also be at the amusement park itself to make sure that the engineering work is done properly. You will even have the chance to do a test ride of the roller coaster yourself. However, this is usually done when the amusement park is closed, so you may find yourself taking a ride at night.

THE ROUTE TO

ROLLER COASTER ENGINEERING

YOU MAY NEED TO STUDY:

SECONDARY SCHOOL: Math, science (especially physics), engineering, and design

POST-SECONDARY: Electrical engineering, civil engineering, or mechanical engineering

WHERE YOU WORK

Some of the bigger amusement parks employ their own roller coaster engineers. They mostly work on the maintenance of the rides that are already there. There are also engineering companies that specialize in designing and building new roller coasters.

▼ Modern roller coaster designs put riders through extreme moves, including loops and corkscrews.

THE FASTEST ROLLER COASTER IS FORMULA ROSSA AT FERRARI WORLD IN THE UNITED ARAB EMIRATES. IT ZOOMS ALONG AT 149 MPH (240 KPH).

ENGINEERING AIRCRAFT

FIND OUT WHAT IT TAKES TO GET THE WIND BENEATH YOUR WINGS.

▼ The Boeing 787 Dreamliner is built from composite materials, making it lighter and more fuel efficient than other airliners.

Aircraft, or **aeronautical**, engineers work on the design, building, and maintenance of all sorts of aircraft. They design the shape of an aircraft so that it will take off, fly through the air, and land. They also make sure that the aircraft is fitted with the right engines, and other systems, such as **navigation** and communication. Above all, they need to make sure that the aircraft is safe and complies with many international **regulations**.

◄ Some aeronautical engineers are involved in the creation of experimental aircraft, such as this X-43A "**scramjet**" tested by NASA.

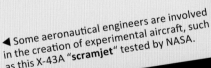

WHAT YOU DO

As an aeronautical engineer, you will spend some time in your office, but there are plenty of times when you will be working elsewhere. You will be in the workshops where the parts of the aircraft are being made, or in the hangers where all the parts are put together. You will also be in the laboratory testing aircraft parts.

AERONAUTICAL ENGINEERS ARE AN IMPORTANT PART OF A CRASH INVESTIGATION TEAM. THEY HELP TO WORK OUT HOW THE CRASH HAPPENED, SO THAT SIMILAR ACCIDENTS CAN BE AVOIDED.

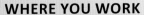

WHERE YOU WORK

Most aeronautical engineers work for companies that design and build aircraft. Airline operators also employ their own aeronautical engineers. If you work for an airline operator, much of your working day will be on the maintenance of the aircraft the operator owns.

◄ Using the latest design technology and materials, future airliners may look very different from those used today.

THE ROUTE TO

YOU MAY NEED TO STUDY:

SECONDARY SCHOOL: Math, science, and engineering

AERONAUTICAL ENGINEERING

POST-SECONDARY: Aeronautical or aerospace engineering, electrical engineering, or mechanical engineering

BUILDING BRIDGES

CUTTING-EDGE ENGINEERING TECHNOLOGY IS USED TO CROSS RIVERS, VALLEYS, AND GORGES.

Your work as a bridge engineer will start well before the design and engineering begins. Your first step will be selecting the correct location, taking into account many variables such as the local geology and weather conditions. You will also have to work with models, usually computer-generated, before the real thing is actually built. As a bridge engineer, you will also have to make sure that your bridges can survive not only the daily use of pedestrians, car, or trains, but also extreme weather conditions such as hurricanes or tornadoes.

THE DANYANG–KUNSHAN GRAND BRIDGE IS THE LONGEST IN THE WORLD, STRETCHING FOR NEARLY 103 MILES (165 KM).

THE ROUTE TO

BRIDGE ENGINEERING

YOU MAY NEED TO STUDY:

SECONDARY SCHOOL: Math, science, computer science, and engineering

POST-SECONDARY: Structural or civil engineering

A BRIDGE IN CHINA IS KNOWN LOCALLY AS "BRAVE MAN'S BRIDGE" BECAUSE THE WALKWAY IS MADE OF GLASS. THIS GIVES USERS A SCARY VIEW OF THE VALLEY FLOOR 590 FEET (180 METERS) BELOW.

▶ A CAD model of a bridge allows engineers to test designs and materials before anything has been built.

WHERE YOU WORK

If you want to work in bridge engineering, you will probably work for a company that specializes in civil engineering projects. Some engineers also work for rail companies or for national organizations that maintain roads. Whoever you work for, you will be working with other engineers and with non–engineers, such as designers and architects.

▼ The Millau **Viaduct** in France is the second-tallest bridge in the world, with towers reaching 1,125 feet (343 meters) high.

WHAT YOU DO

Bridge engineers divide their time between their office, the laboratory, and the site where the bridge is located. In the office, you will spend your time working on the engineering needed for a new bridge. This will include creating computer models to test how the bridge will work. In the laboratory, you will help in the construction of models to carry on with testing. You will supervise the building of the bridge, and may also be involved in checking the bridge at regular intervals after its opening.

GLOSSARY

ADDITIVE MANUFACTURING
Another term for 3-D printing, it refers to how objects are made by adding material, such as plastic and metal, rather than by starting with a large block of material and cutting pieces away to make the object.

AERODYNAMICS
The study of how air moves around solid objects

AERONAUTICAL
Related to the design and study of machines that can fly

AMUSEMENT PARK
A large park that contains rides, such as roller coasters, and game stalls to entertain people

AQUIFER
An underground layer of rock that contains a large quantity of water and can be used to supply wells

ARCHITECT
A person who designs buildings

BIOENGINEER
A person who designs replacement body parts, such as artificial limbs

CIVIL ENGINEERING
The design and building of large engineering projects, such as harbors, roads, bridges, and public buildings

CLIMATE CHANGE
The change in Earth's overall climate which many scientists believe is being caused by human activities

COMPUTER-AIDED DESIGN
Using computer software and graphics to design objects, such as cars, aircraft, and buildings

DOCTORATE
One of the highest education qualifications students can receive

FORMULA ONE
The highest class of car racing for professional drivers

FRICTION
A force produced when one surface or object rubs against another

GAIT ANALYSIS
The study of how a person walks or runs; It is used to see how an athlete can improve their performance.

GEOLOGY
The study of the history and structure of Earth, in particular its rocks

GORGE
A very steep-sided valley that's usually formed by the eroding actions of a river

GRAND PRIX
The races that make up a season in Formula One car racing

GREENHOUSE GASES
The gases that add to the greenhouse effect and may cause climate change

HYDROELECTRIC POWER
Electricity that's generated by the movement of water

MASTER'S DEGREE
A university degree that is a higher level than a bachelor's degree

MUD LOG
A record of the soil and rock brought to the surface by drilling

NAVIGATION
The ability to find your location and plot a route to another location

PROSTHETICS
Artificial body parts that are used to replace natural parts that are damaged or have been lost

REGULATIONS
Rules and principles that govern how something should behave

RENEWABLE ENERGY
Electricity that is produced from sources that won't run out, such as the wind, waves, and sunlight

ROLLER COASTER
Open cars that run on rails and go through a series of moves intended to thrill or scare the riders, such as steep drops, loops, and corkscrews

SCRAMJET
A type of jet engine that is designed to cope with very fast speeds

SHIPYARD
A place where ships are built, maintained, or repaired

SOLAR FARM
Also known as a photovoltaic power station; This is an area of land that is covered with solar cells which generate electricity from sunlight.

TURBINE
A large wheel that is made up of a series of blades

VIADUCT
A bridge that carries a road or railway across a valley

WIND TURBINE
A generator that produces electricity when the wind turns its bladed wheel

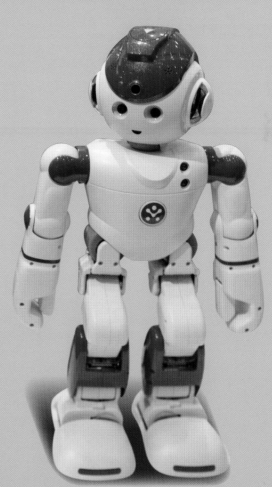

INDEX